If I Had a Hammer

WOODWORKING
WITH SEVEN
BASIC TOOLS
Robert Lasson

photographs by Jeff Murphy

E. P. DUTTON & CO., INC.   NEW YORK

Library of Congress Cataloging in Publication Data

Lasson, Robert   If I had a hammer

SUMMARY: Text and photographs introduce seven hand tools
and give instructions for six woodworking projects using them.

1. Woodwork—Juvenile literature.   [1. Woodwork]
I. Murphy, Jeff, illus.   II. Title.
TT185.L33   684'.082   74-6457   ISBN 0-525-32532-8

Published simultaneously in Canada by Clarke,
Irwin & Company Limited, Toronto and Vancouver

Designed by Riki Levinson
Printed in the U.S.A.   First Edition
10 9 8 7 6 5 4 3 2 1

Contents

A Note for Parents

This book features seven relatively inexpensive hand tools. The opening section shows, in text and photos, how to use them. The following section describes six projects that can be built with these tools. Most important, as beginning woodworkers learn the capabilities of each tool, they can eventually build anything they want with them.

There's an important rule for buying tools: get the most expensive tool you can afford. You can, however, cut some corners. For example, you don't have to spend $4.00 for a try square. Cheaper squares are available and will be adequate.

You may already own a brace-and-bit or an electric drill, which means you may not wish to buy a hand drill. (Electric drills should be operated *only* by adults until the beginning woodworker has had a chance to develop familiarity with power-driven equipment—and a great deal of respect for it.)

The Surform plane, tape measure, and C-clamp all cost around $3.00 or less. No skimping is necessary. Two items *not* to skimp on are the saw and the hammer. A cheap saw is really worse than no saw at all because it cuts poorly and frustrates anyone who tries to use it. A decent 20-inch crosscut saw like the one shown in the book can be had for as little as $6.00.

The hammer is also important. Under no circumstances should you buy the cheap cast-iron hammers sold in the five-and-dime stores. These hammers are actually dangerous because pieces of the head tend to chip and fly off in use. The hammer shown costs around $4.00. It is a 10-ounce model, as opposed to the standard 16-ounce hammer, which is too heavy for, say, a ten-year-old to handle proficiently.

Although a workbench is not an absolute necessity, you do need some sort of table or working surface that's about mid-thigh high to the young woodworker. This surface should be heavy enough so that wood can be clamped to it and sawed and drilled without wobbling. Of course, if you already have a workbench with a vise attached, you're ahead of the game. The C-clamp is a workable substitute, but not as versatile as a vise. On the other hand, a decent woodworking vise costs about five times as much as a clamp.

Ideally, the working place should be located away from living quarters. Garage, basement, carport are all fine—but not the family room. The decorator magazines often show cute workbenches in living or family rooms, but in real life this is completely impractical. The working place should be just that: a place for working with wood—which means making noise and raising dust—a place where tools and lumber and partially finished projects may be left safely. It may be small, but the working place should have good light, either natural or artificial; and it should be dry.

Finishing—sanding, staining, painting, and the like—can be done out of doors on a porch, patio, or driveway. Surfaces to be protected should be covered with newspapers held down with rocks.

Practice—lots of practice—is needed before anyone can use tools adeptly. Your role should be helpful and supportive, while always allowing the young woodworker to move ahead at his or her own speed. The human hand is itself a magnificent tool, but sometimes two aren't enough. If your child needs help —that is, if he/she *asks* for assistance—give it. This book is predicated on child-to-child or child-to-adult collaboration.

R. L.

1

The Hammer

The hammer is used to drive nails, to remove nails, and to tap pieces of wood into place before nailing. The hammer your father uses is called a 16-ounce hammer because that's what the metal head weighs. That hammer is probably too heavy for you. So the hammer shown and used here is a 10-ounce hammer.

How to start a nail: hold the nail near the pointed end and place it in position on the wood. With the nail held straight up, tap the nailhead gently with your hammer two or three times. Once the nail is in far enough to stand up by itself, take your fingers away from the nail.

Hold the hammer where the handle feels most comfortable. Drive the nail down with slow, steady swings. Don't try to see how *fast* you can put the nail in. Just try to get it in straight.

When the nail is almost completely in, make your final hits lighter so that the hammerhead does not dent your wood.

If the nail starts to bend, stop hammering and pull it out right away. A block of wood placed under the hammerhead, as shown in the top photograph on page 5, will give you better leverage and make your job easier. Don't use the old nail hole again. Start the new nail in a new place.

Fingers get banged when your holding hand is too close to the nail. When the nail stands up by itself, you will have to hold the piece of wood with your free hand. But keep that hand well away from the nail. And swing your hammer slowly but firmly.

It takes practice to use the hammer properly. Try hammering nails into scraps of wood, making each swing and grip a little different. In this way, you'll find the grip that works best for you.

Careful: *Never* leave pieces of wood around that have nails sticking through them. Either pull the nails out or bend them over so that they can't hurt anyone.

Full-size hammer (below right) weighs 16 ounces and is 13¾″ long. It is too heavy for most young people to use. A more comfortable size is shown at left. It weighs only 10 ounces and is 12½″ long.

When you start a nail, hold the nail on the wood and tap it lightly with the hammer until the nail stands by itself.

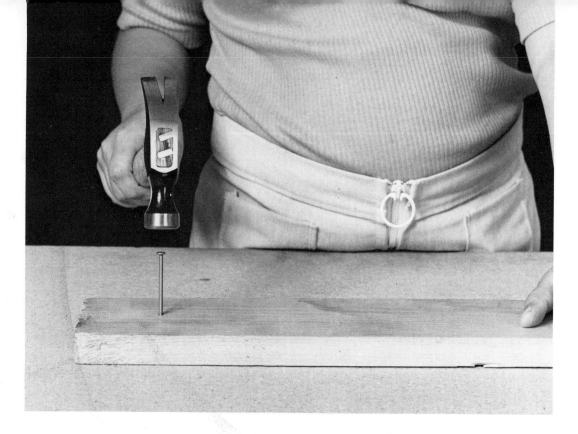

When the nail stands up, move your hand away and start hammering the nail in deeper. Hold the hammer handle where it feels most comfortable for you.

It happens to the best of us. When a nail bends, don't try to straighten it. Just pull it out right away.

A block of wood under the hammerhead makes the nail easier to pull out. Hold the handle at the end. Pull it toward you with a slow, steady movement and the nail will lift out easily. Don't start another nail in the same hole or the new nail will probably bend, too.

Try hammering nails into scraps of wood for practice, making each swing and grip a little different. Nails should be removed or bent over when you're finished.

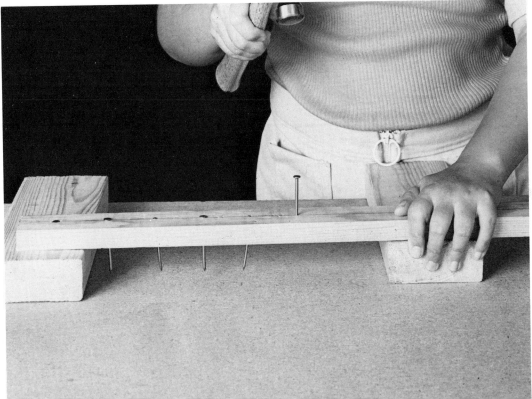

The Try Square

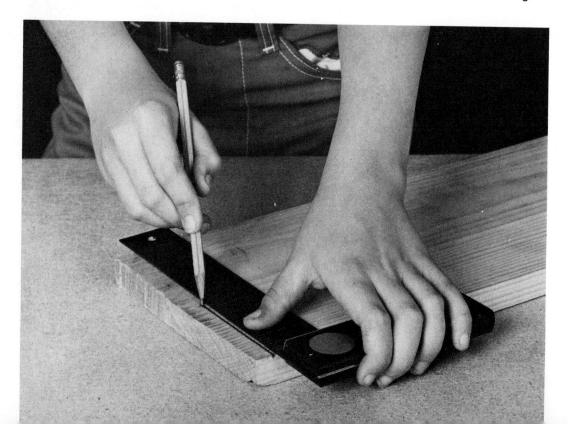

The try square is a steel-and-wood measure that helps you do accurate work. You use it to mark wood for cutting, to see if a board is warped or not, and to check how accurately you've joined two pieces of wood together. Also, since the metal part is marked off in inches, the try square is a handy ruler.

Boards often come with ragged or unsquare ends that must be removed. To put a square end on these pieces, hold your try square firmly against one edge and draw your line for sawing. Don't make the line too close to end or you'll have a hard time sawing.

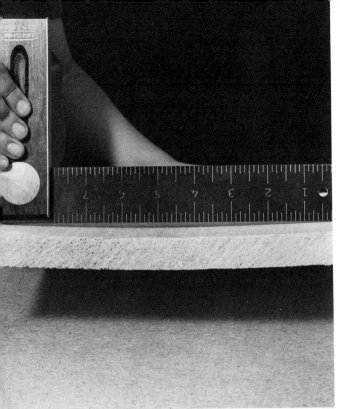

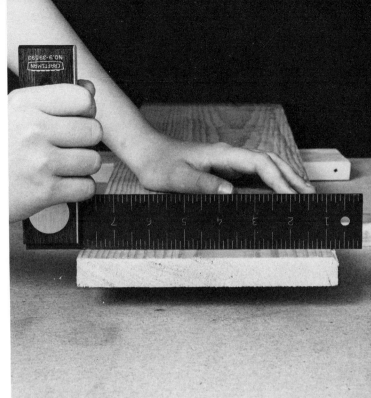

Above: The try square shows that this piece of wood is badly warped, and not good to build with.

Above right: This piece of wood, on the other hand, is completely free of warp. This is the kind you want to buy.

One of the best uses of the try square is for checking how well you have joined two pieces of wood. When you hold your square firmly against one piece, it should fit snugly against both. This is a good joint.

The Saw

Since all of the sawing in this book is done across the grain, we use a crosscut saw. It has teeth specially made for this purpose. A rip saw, made to cut *with* the grain, has its teeth set somewhat differently.

The crosscut saw shown is called a 20-inch saw. It is shorter than the full-size saw adults use, and a bit easier to handle.

Making a straight saw cut takes practice. Don't be discouraged when you have trouble at first. The more you use the saw, the better you'll get.

Wood to be sawed should be clamped to your work surface. And you should always saw along a pencil line, not freehand.

To start, place the back teeth of the saw (near the handle) on your mark. Pull the saw toward you, guiding it with your thumb. *Notice that the thumb is held above the teeth* on the smooth part of the saw. The first stroke toward you will make a small nick in the wood. Now, lift the saw completely from the wood and place the back teeth in the nick again. Pull the saw toward you again, and then push it away from you. The saw should now start cutting.

Use a smooth push-pull action. Quick or jerky movements only cause bad cuts. If your arm gets tired, just stop sawing and take a rest. Hold the saw straight and always keep your eye on the pencil line.

If you have a helper, ask him or her to blow the sawdust away so that you can see the line clearly. If the saw goes off the line, twist the handle gently in the direction you want it to go. As you reach the end of your cut, make slower strokes. Ask your helper to hold the end being cut off so that it does not break off or splinter.

A crosscut saw should be used only on wood. Be careful of cutting into knots. Knots are very hard and can damage your saw teeth. When planning cuts, draw your pencil lines so that you avoid cutting through knots.

When your saw is not in use, hang it on a peg or nail. Or store it where other metal tools will not hit against the blade.

Saw teeth are small but very sharp. Always keep your fingers away from that part of the saw.

Wood to be sawed should be clamped down and marked with a pencil line. To begin, hold the saw on the line. As your thumb guides the blade above the teeth, pull the saw toward you at the angle shown. Remove the saw from the little nick you have made and repeat the motion. The saw should now start cutting, and you can begin a steady push-pull action.

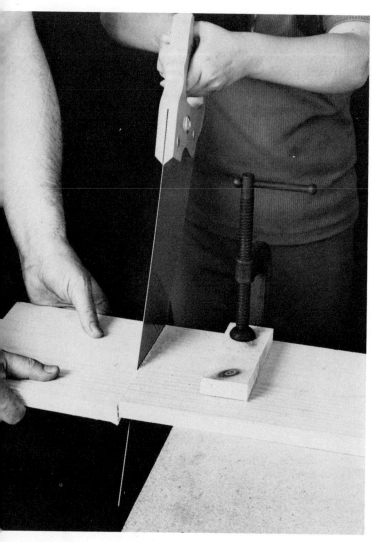

A partner is helpful for blowing away sawdust so that you can see the pencil line. Also for holding the cut-off piece to prevent it from breaking off or splintering. Always slow down your sawing movements when you get near the end.

As you learn to saw, check your progress with a try square. The saw should be perfectly straight, not at an angle like this.

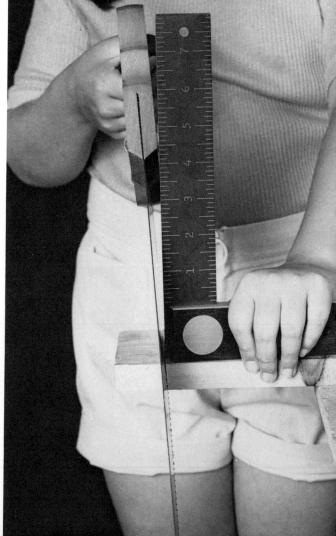

The C-Clamp

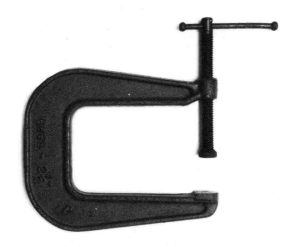

If you don't have a vise, you'll need a C-clamp to hold wood while you're sawing, drilling, or planing. A useful size is a 3-inch deep throat. You should have a 5-inch clamp too.

Always protect your work with a piece of scrap wood. If you don't, the clamp will bite into your work and leave deep, round marks that are impossible to get rid of.

When you adjust your clamp, it should be just tight enough to hold your work firmly. A few drops of oil on the metal threads will make the handle easier to turn.

The C-clamp is like a third hand. It holds your work steady when you're sawing, drilling, or planing. Never tighten the clamp directly onto your work.

The Tape Measure

You must measure your wood very carefully, or the pieces will not fit. Most often wood is wasted because of careless or inaccurate measuring. That's why old-time woodworkers say, "Measure twice, cut once." Always double-check a measurement before you make your cut.

The roll-up steel tape measure is the handiest measuring tool. It stretches as long as you need it, yet fits in your pocket. It won't break (unless you really work at it). Also, the tape measure has a steel L on the end that hooks it over the end of a board. It's like an extra hand when you really need it.

When you measure, hold the tape firmly along one edge of your board. If you hold it diagonally, your measurement will not be accurate.

The sign for inch is ". When you see a measurement of 6", that means six inches. The sign for foot is '. Therefore, 2' 3" means two feet, three inches.

You can buy a tape measure as long as 14', but a 10' or 12' tape is long enough. A foot is divided into twelve inches. Most of the measurements in this book are in full inches, or ¼", ½", ¾", to make your measuring easy.

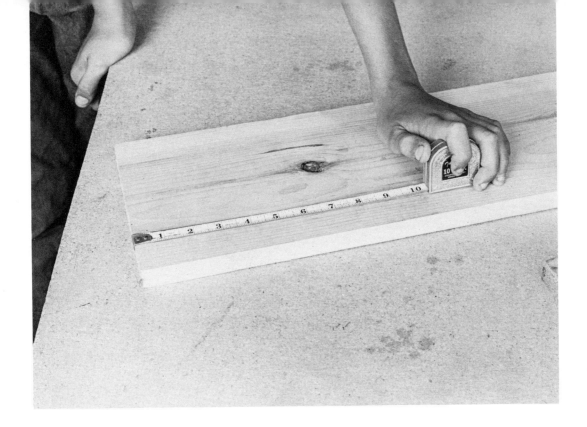

Hold your tape measure along one edge of the board, with the L hooked firmly over the end. Keep the tape straight. If it's at an angle, your measurement will be off.

Make your mark near the edge of the board.

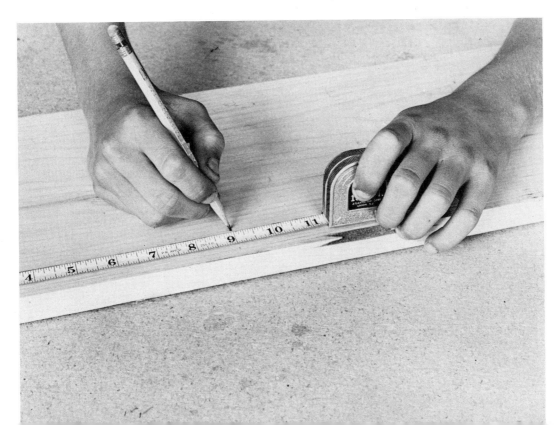

Move your try square up to the mark and draw your pencil line. Leave a little space between the mark and the try square for the thickness of the pencil point.

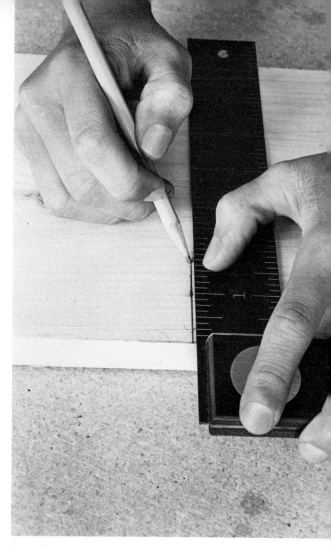

The steel tape is also designed for taking inside measurements. Hold the tape as shown, read the ruler, and add two inches for the length of the tape casing. This gives you the exact inside measurement.

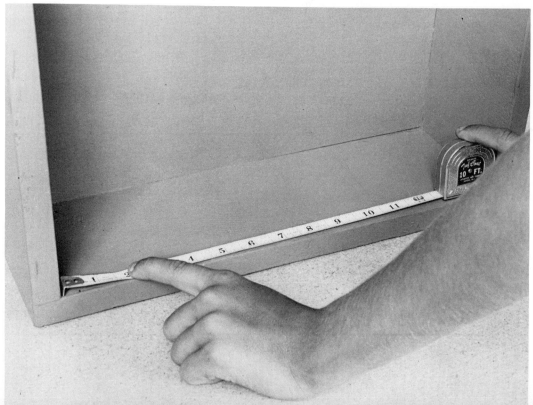

The Drill

The drill is a tool for making holes in wood. The drill has a handle that turns a gear, a chuck to hold cutting bits or twist drills, and two knobs to help you keep the drill straight.

With drill bits that fit into the chuck, you can make holes up to ¼″ diameter with this drill.

To insert a bit, lock the gear handle with your thumb, as shown on page 16. Rotate the chuck until the bit fits between the jaws. Push the bit into the chuck as far as it will go. Now close the jaws by turning the chuck in the opposite direction, still locking the handle so that the gear cannot move. Tighten the chuck as hard as you can.

To remove the bit, lock the gear handle and turn the chuck in the opposite direction until the jaws open.

When drilling, hold the drill straight up and down, not at an angle. If you don't, your hole will not be straight. Always hold the drill firmly by one of the knob handles. If the drill wobbles around while you're using it, your bit may break off.

The drill shown in this book is a British import, Record Ridgway #423. It is available in the United States through Woodcraft Supply Corp., 313 Montvale Ave., Woburn, Mass. 01801. You can write directly to this company for price and availability.

It is a sturdy, rugged tool, requiring some strength to operate. Don't press down too hard, but keep the gear turning at a steady rate. It turns *away* from you. Let the bit do the work, not your pressure.

When the hole is finished, here's how to remove the drill.

Do *not* turn the gear in the opposite direction. Keep turning it just as if you were drilling—*away* from you. But start pulling the drill gently upward at the same time. The bit will lift out of the hole.

If you have to make a ¼″ hole, do it in two steps. First, make a hole with a smaller bit—⅛″ or ¹¹⁄₃₂″ is good. Then remove that bit, insert your ¼″ bit, and enlarge the hole you just made. The larger bit will automatically find the center of the first hole. You'll find this much easier than trying to drill with the ¼″ bit right from the start.

Work to be drilled should be clamped in a "sandwich." Put one scrap under your work, your work in the middle, and another piece of scrap on top. The bottom scrap protects your work surface and also prevents the hole from having rough splinters. The top piece protects the work from clamp marks.

To insert a drill bit (the part that makes the holes), lock the gear handle with your thumb. Rotate the chuck until the three steel jaws open wide enough to hold the bit.

Put the bit into the chuck as far as it will go. To tighten, keep the gear handle locked. Rotate the chuck in the opposite direction as hard as you can. The supplier of this drill is given on page 15.

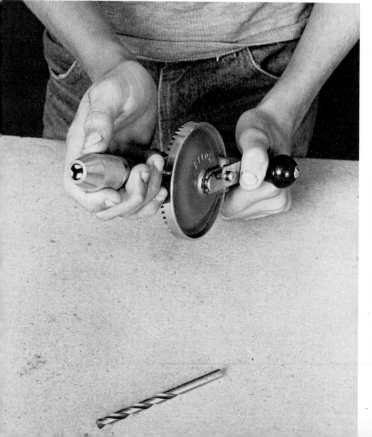
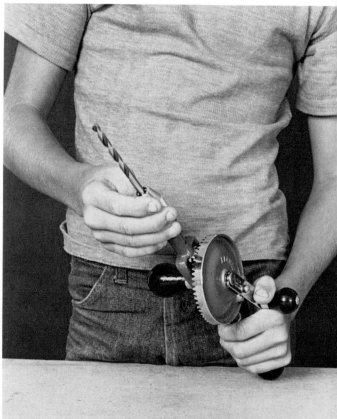

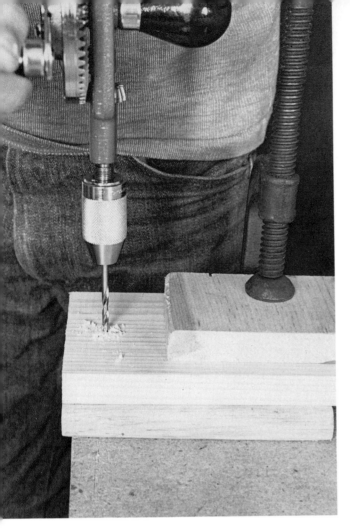

Drilling a ¼″ hole is done in two steps. First, clamp your work in a "sandwich" between two pieces of scrap lumber. Then make a hole with a ⅛″ or ¹¹⁄₃₂″ bit. To remove the drill, turn the gear away from you as you pull the drill gently upward.

Now finish the job by enlarging the smaller hole with a ¼″ bit. Drilling by hand is not as easy as it looks. Don't press down too hard, but keep the gear handle turning at a steady rate. Always hold the drill straight, or you may snap off your bit.

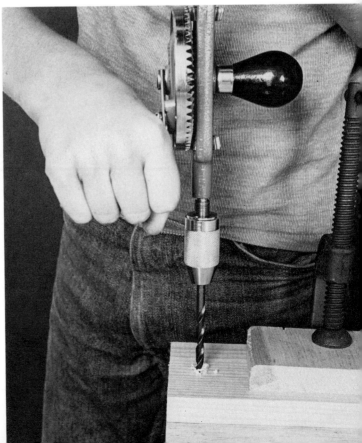

The hole at the left was made in a "sandwich." The one at the right was made while the work stuck out over the end of the work surface. Quite a difference.

Simple bit-holder. Drill holes part way into a piece of 2 x 3. Put the drills in their own holes. All bits have their sizes stamped into the upper ends. Mark down the sizes so you know what's where.

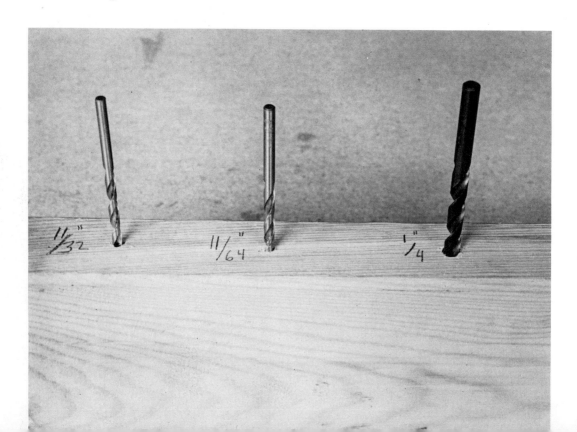

The Surform Plane

This tool is more like a file or wood rasp, and easier to use than a standard woodworking plane. Use it to smooth sides and ends of pieces, to smooth off sharp edges, or even to make round corners.

The Surform® plane works best when your work is clamped firmly in place. Or with a "stop block" nailed to your work surface, as shown in the photograph below. The stop block is a piece of 1″ x 1″ wood nailed to the bench. Nails are bent over on the underside of the bench. Place your work squarely against it.

This plane works with or against the grain and requires pressure and elbow grease, so don't be afraid to press down with it. Try it out on scrap pieces to get the feel of it. When the cutting edge of your plane gets dull, replace the blade.

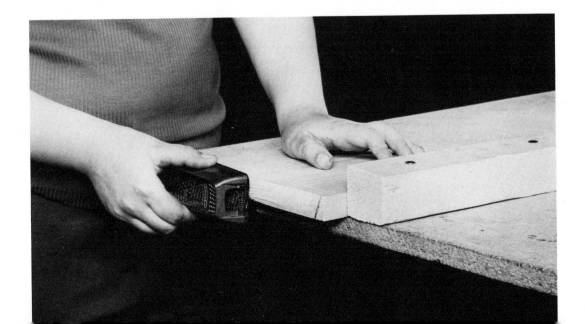

HOW TO MAKE ROUND CORNERS

Measure 1″ from the corner in both directions and make your marks. Connect marks with pencil line to form triangle. Saw off the corner.

With work clamped down, start rounding the corner with your plane.

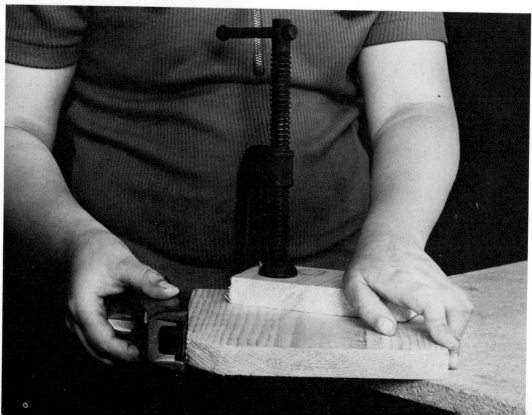

Smooth rough areas with medium-grade sandpaper. Use a rubber sandpaper block or fit sandpaper around a piece of wood.

The finished round corner, and the plane that made it.

Some Tips on Lumber

Lumber is cut into boards from 2″ to 12″ wide, in even-numbered jumps. We use 1″ x 4″, 1″ x 6″, 1″ x 8″, and 2″ x 3″. The "x" means "by," so these figures are read as "one by four," "one by six," and so on.

The first numeral tells the thickness of the board. The second numeral tells the width of the board. So a 1″ x 8″ is 1 inch thick by 8 inches wide.

But when you go to buy a 1″ x 8″, you'll find that it is really less than 1 inch thick and less than 8 inches wide. The board *was* that big when it was first cut. But after the board was dried in a large oven and then planed down, it shrank to about ¾″ thick by 7⅝″ wide. However, we still call it a 1″ x 8″.

Lumber is sold in even-numbered lengths, usually beginning with 4′. After that, you can buy boards that are 6′, 8′, 10′, all the way to 18′ long. When you build something, you have to figure out how many feet you'll actually need, and then buy the nearest even-numbered amount. For example, if you need 8½′ you'll have to buy 10′ of lumber—8′ would not be enough, and you can't buy 9′. So you have to buy 10′.

The lumber shown in this book is called Number 2 pine. This should be pretty straight and free from warp. If it has knots, they should be tight. Large, loose knots should be avoided, because they will fall out. Knots in general are very hard to cut through and impossible to nail. So be choosy when you go to buy lumber. Look through the pile until you find what you want. Make sure the ends of the boards are not cracked or split.

All lumber has grain, which is a pattern caused by the tree's growth. In boards, the grain runs lengthwise. The sawing in this book is done across the grain.

Above: Although the top board is called a 1" x 8", it really measures less. That's because it was dried and planed after it was first cut. A 1" x 8" actually measures from 7¼" to 7⅝" wide. This 1" x 10" is not even 9½" wide. But we still call them 1" x 8" and 1" x 10".

Above right: So-called 1" boards are closer to ¾" in thickness.

Number 2 pine will have knots, but they should be firm, like those in the bottom piece. Don't buy lumber with loose knots because they will fall out. Boards with too many knots should also be avoided. Knots are very hard to saw through and impossible to nail.

How to Assemble
Two Pieces of Wood

Almost anything you make requires nailing two pieces of wood together. It's not hard to do, but things can go wrong if you're not careful. First, you have to make sure that the nails you use are not too short to hold the pieces of wood together, or so long that they split the wood or come out the other side.

Another thing to remember: when you nail a thin and thick piece together, you always nail the thin wood to the thick wood. This gives the nail more wood to sink into and to hold tight.

Be careful to place the nail correctly. If you nail too close to the outer edge, your nail will stick out the side of the wood. The same thing happens if you nail too close to the inner edge. To avoid this, mark the thickness of your wood. You can begin driving your nails on your work surface. Drive them until they just begin to come through the other side.

Then put the first piece of wood carefully over the piece you are nailing into. A helper to hold your bottom piece of wood is very handy at this stage. When both pieces are exactly where you want them, start hammering your nails. But do not hammer the nails all the way in until you are sure that the nails will not split the wood or come out where you don't want them to. When you have checked this, drive the nails all the way in.

Nails   There are two kinds of nails used in this book—"common" and "finishing."

The common nail has a large flat head which is easy to hit with a hammer. But the nailhead will show after the nail is driven in.

The finishing nail has a much smaller head. It can be hammered into the wood so that the head does not show as much.

Use common nails when it doesn't matter if the nailheads

show. Or when you plan to paint over them. Use finishing nails for finer work or for projects that you will stain or shellac.

Woodworkers (and hardware dealers) don't call nails 2″ or 3″ nails, but rather 6-penny or 8-penny nails. Years ago, you bought a hundred nails for four pennies or six pennies or eight pennies, depending on the size. Naturally, the smaller nails cost fewer pennies. We still talk of nail sizes in this way, even though you now buy nails by the pound or by the box.

The projects shown in this book use 6- or 8-penny common and finishing nails.

Glue If you use glue, apply it to both surfaces of the wood to be nailed together; this makes a stronger joint. Spread the glue with a popsicle stick or a scrap of wood. Then nail the pieces of wood together.

Do not use too much glue. If some oozes out when you hammer in your nails, wipe it off. This white glue, Elmer's, is made for things to be used *inside* the house only. For outside projects you must use waterproof glue.

FOUR MISTAKES IN ASSEMBLING TWO PIECES OF WOOD (AND HOW TO AVOID THEM)

1. This 8-penny nail is too long and too thick for this job. It has already split the top piece and is beginning to split the bottom one.

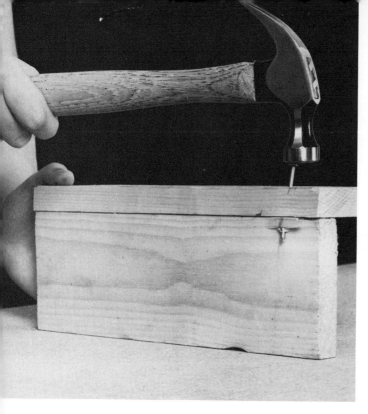 

2. Nail is the right size, but it is too close to the outer edge.

3. Nail is the right size, but it is too close to the inner edge.

4. Nail is the right size and did not split the wood. But it was hammered in before the worker checked the position of the pieces. They should be flush. Never drive nails all the way in until the pieces are in their correct positions.

HOW TO MAKE BETTER JOINTS

The bottom board is to be nailed to the top one. Find the thickness of the wood by holding it as shown and drawing a pencil line. Your line should be drawn lightly, as pencil lines are hard to remove.

Now that you see what the thickness is, start your nails in the center of the nailing area. Don't nail too close to the ends. And don't keep your holding hand too close to the nail you're hammering.

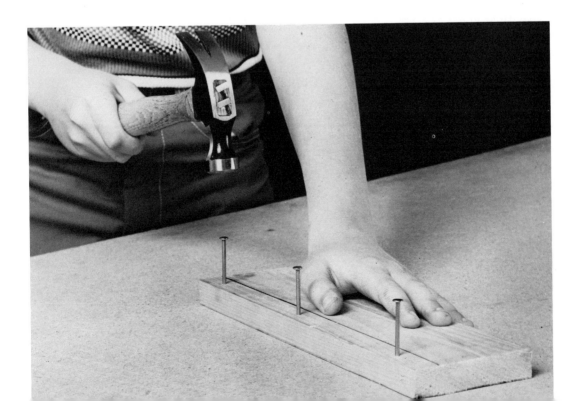

Above: Drive in the nails until the points just start to come through the other side. Then stop.

Above right: As your helper gives you a hand holding the work, drive in the first nail part way. Then, lining up the back, drive another nail part way. When you're sure that the position of both pieces is correct, drive the nails in all the way.

A good rule to remember: When you have to join a thin piece and a thick piece, nail the thin into the thick. If you do it the other way, the nail will not hold well, as you can see.

At left of photograph, 6-penny common and finishing nails are shown. At right, 8-penny common and finishing nails. The common nails are easier to hammer, but their heads can be seen in a finished project.

Below: In some projects, glue will also be called for. Squeeze the glue from the container in a thin, steady stream.

Below right: With a popsicle stick or piece of scrap, spread the glue over the entire surface. Excess glue that oozes out after you hammer should be wiped away. If you let it dry, it will spoil your finish.

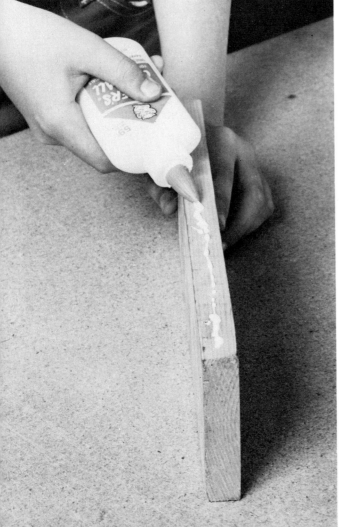

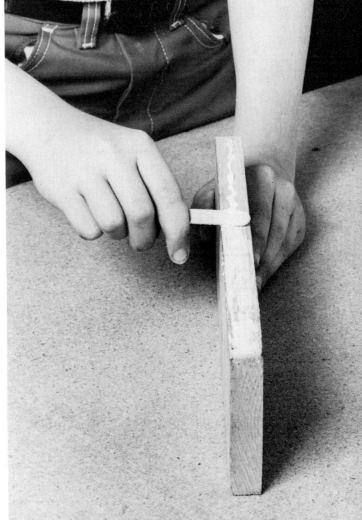

Potholder Hanger

Easy-to-make hanger holds three potholders and will look nice in any kitchen. The hanger is held up with two picture hooks.

Lumber

1″ x 4″
   1 piece, 12″ long

Hardware

3 1″ shoulder hooks
2 decorative rings
2 picture hooks (for hanging)

You can turn a single piece of wood and some brass hardware into a handsome hanger for potholders. It will look attractive in any kitchen.

All the wood you need is 12″ of 1″ x 4″. The brass loops that screw into the top are called decorative rings. The L-shaped hooks are called 1″ shoulder hooks. They can be all bought at the five-and-dime.

L-shaped shoulder hooks work better than curved cup hooks because the potholders are easier to put on and take off.

Begin by cutting your wood to 12″. Now measure where the rings and hooks will go. The rings are placed 1½″ from either end of the wood. Place the rings toward the back edge of the wood. This makes the hanger lie flat against the wall. When you've marked off where the rings are to go, take a 6-penny common nail and make small starter holes by hammering the nail ¼″ into the wood. Then take out the nail.

Now for the shoulder hooks. All three hooks are located 1½″ from the bottom of the rack. The center hook is right in the center of the board, 6″ from either end. The end hooks are 2″ from each end. Mark these positions with small crosses, as shown on page 34 (bottom). Pencil marks should be drawn lightly because they are very hard to sand off. And if you stain your potholder hanger, as this one has been, the pencil lines will show through unless they have been sanded away.

When the places for the three hooks are marked, make starter holes with your nail again, as you did for the ring holes.

You now have a piece of wood with five starter holes—two holes for the rings and three for the hooks. Now, to make the hanger look a little more interesting, round off the four front corners with your plane. You probably won't need the C-clamp for this job. When the corners are rounded the way you want them, you're ready to finish the piece.

Do not screw in the rings or hooks until the hanger has been varnished. Sand it down with medium sandpaper, especially the pencil lines. Wipe off all dust with a clean cloth. The holder shown was given two coats of varnish stain. This colors the wood and also gives the rack a slight gloss.

When your varnish is totally dry, screw in the hooks and rings. Attach your hanger to the kitchen wall with a pair of picture hooks.

Materials: one 12″ piece of 1″ x 4″, two decorative rings, and three 1″ shoulder hooks are all you need to make the potholder hanger.

Above: After cutting wood to 12", measure off positions of decorative rings: 1½" from each end and toward the back edge. Tap a 6-penny common nail ¼" into the wood to make starter holes. Put the ring in the hole, turn a few twists, then remove.

Below: Locate positions for shoulder hooks with crosses. All holes should be 1½" from bottom. One is centered, 6" from each end; the others are 2" from each end. Keep your pencil marks small and light. Make starter holes first with a nail.

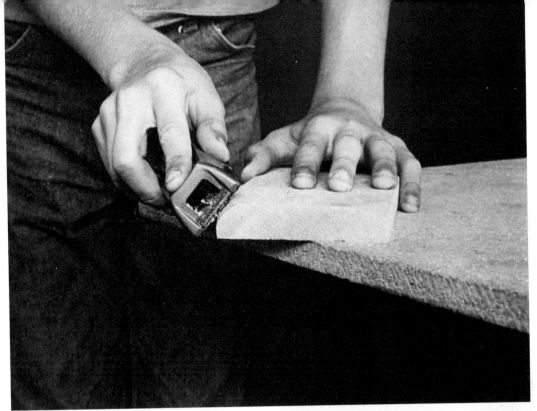

Round off the four front corners with your plane. You probably won't need the C-clamp for this job.

Smooth down the entire piece, including edges, with medium-grade sandpaper. The pencil marks should be sanded off completely, and the hanger may then be stained or varnished. When the varnish is dry, screw in all the hooks and rings. Then attach your hanger in a handy spot in the kitchen.

Desktop Book Rack

Handy desktop book rack holds books neatly on any desk or table. This rack is made of 1″ x 8″ pine.

Lumber
1″ x 8″
  1 bottom, 15″ long
  2 ends, 6½″ each
Total Lumber
28″

Fastening
6 6-penny finishing nails
glue

All you need to make this useful book rack are three short pieces of 1″ x 8″ pine, some glue, and six 6-penny finishing nails. The tops of the end pieces may be cut diagonally, or you can round them off. (The section, How to Make Round Corners, pages 20-21, explains how this is done.)

Begin by cutting your pieces to size. The bottom piece is 15″ long. The end pieces are 6½″ long. When the corners of the ends are cut or rounded off, you're ready to fasten the three pieces together. First put a light coating of glue on one end of the bottom piece. Spread the glue evenly with a popsicle stick or a thin piece of wood.

Begin hammering three 6-penny finishing nails along the bottom of one end piece. Hammer the nails on your work surface until the points just start to come through. Apply glue to the lower inside edge of the end piece. Then ask your helper to hold the bottom piece so that its glued end is up.

Position the end piece exactly where you want it, and start hammering the nails all the way in. Do the same for the other end—and that's all there is to making your book rack.

Give the glue a chance to dry. It's best to leave anything glued to dry overnight before you handle it. If you keep lifting the glued piece and checking it, the glue will not set properly.

The next day, you can sand down your book rack with medium-grade sandpaper and stain or paint the rack. The rack shown here was stained with light brown Minwax, which gives a dull finish. If you want a finish that's a little more shiny, use a varnish stain.

The bottom of the rack is 15″ long. The ends are 6½″ long. You can round off the corners of the end pieces, as shown at left. Or just make straight diagonal cuts (at right), 1″ in either direction from the corner.

When all three pieces are cut, fix the corners the way you want them, diagonal or rounded. Spread a light coating of glue on one end of the bottom piece. Start driving the nails on your work surface until the points come through the end piece. Apply glue to the end piece. While your helper holds the bottom piece straight up, hammer the nails all the way in. Do the same for the other end piece, and that's it!

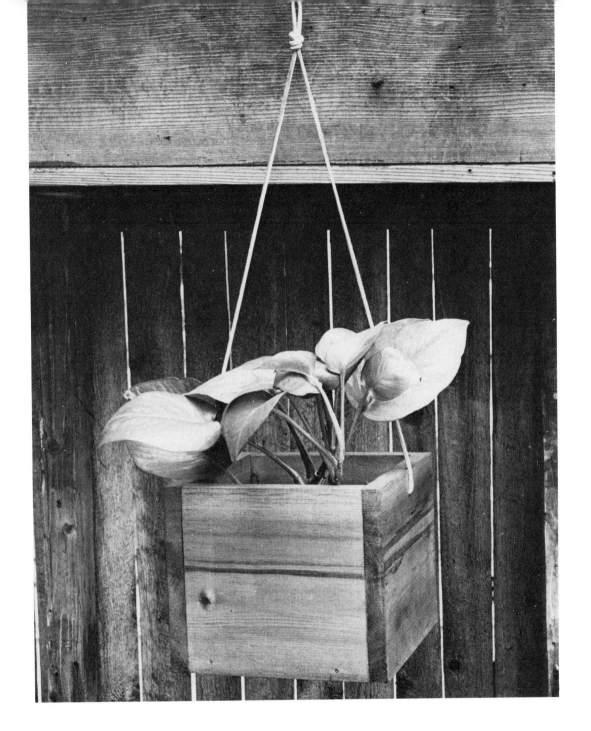

Hanging Planter

Planter is made from 1″ x 8″ pine and hung outdoors with a leather thong. Flower pot sits inside, and a hole in the bottom lets out excess water.

Lumber

1" x 8"

   1 bottom, 7¼" long
     (or as long as the lumber is wide)
   2 short sides, 7¼" each
   2 long sides, 8¾" each

Total Lumber

39¼"

Fastening

12 6-penny common or finishing nails

3' to 4' of heavy twine or leather thong,
   depending on how planter will be hung

This planter is an open box, with two holes in the sides for the twine or leather thong to hang it.

The box is made of a bottom, two short sides, and two long sides. It is designed to hold a flower pot that contains a plant. Don't put earth into the planter, because that will make it too moist and the wood may warp. However, do make a hole in the bottom so that excess water or rain can drain out.

The planter shown was made to hold a 6" flower pot, so the lumber is 1" x 8". If you want to use a smaller pot, 1" x 6" will be satisfactory.

Begin by cutting the bottom piece. This is exactly as long as your lumber is wide. If your 8" lumber measures 7¼" wide, cut off a piece 7¼" long for your bottom. It should be a perfect square.

Now drill the drain hole. First find the exact center of the piece. This is done by drawing diagonal lines from corner to corner. Where the lines cross is the center. Drill your hole, first with a smaller bit, then with a ¼" bit, as shown in the photographs on page 17.

Now cut the two short sides. These are exactly the same size as the bottom. You can use your bottom piece to measure them.

Nail the two short sides to the bottom, making sure that all ends are flush. Use 6-penny common nails or finishing nails, whichever you prefer. If you plan to stain the planter, finishing nails will look better. If you paint it, common nails will be fine.

When the short sides are nailed on, measure for the two

long sides. Be sure to measure along the bottom of the planter, not the top, as the short sides may turn either in or out.

When your long sides are cut, drill ¼″ holes that will hold the twine or thong. Find the center of the side piece, and measure 1″ down from the top. It will save you time to make holes in both side pieces at once, as shown on page 45 (top).

Now attach the long sides, nailing into the bottom and the short sides. Before driving the nails all the way in, be sure the pieces fit properly. Also, *be sure that both twine holes are at the top.*

When the long sides have been nailed, your planter is finished. If the planter will be used out of doors, it must be finished with an exterior paint or exterior stain. If it will be used indoors, you may use interior finishes. The planter shown was finished with an exterior stain that had a slight green tinge. Other colors are also available. Paint or stain the inside as well as the outside.

The bottom of the planter and the two short sides are perfect squares, cut as long as your lumber is wide. Use finishing nails if you stain the planter. Common nails may be used if you paint it.

Drain hole is drilled in the center of the bottom piece. Draw diagonal lines from corners to find center cross mark.

The two short sides are exactly the same size as the bottom. Here they are nailed with 6-penny finishing nails. Make sure that side and bottom edges meet perfectly before you drive nails all the way in. To measure for the long sides, set planter flat on a table. Measure along bottom edge.

The two long sides are drilled with a ¼"
bit. The holes will hold the thong or twine.
Each hole is in the middle of the board and
1" down from the top. Notice the direction
of the grain.

Nail the two long sides to the bottom and to
the short sides. Be sure both thong holes
are at the top. This completes construc-
tion. Now you are ready for finishing.

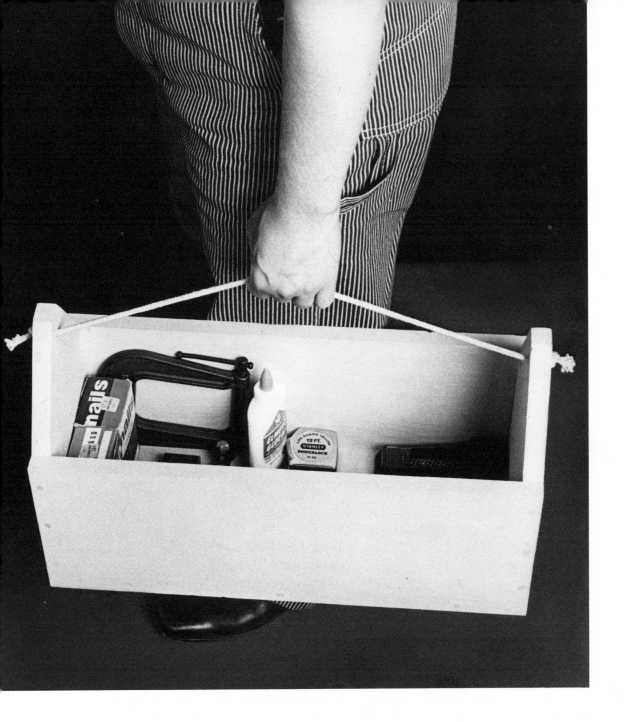

Handy Carrier

Carrier holds tools, hardware, or perhaps hobby equipment. It is made entirely of ¾″ wood. However, if your lumber yard carries ½″ lumber, you can make both sides from that. It will be easier to carry.

Lumber
1″ x 8″
   1 bottom, 18″ long
   2 ends, 11″ each
   2 sides, 19½″ each
Total Lumber
79″

Fastening
24 8-penny common nails
26″ of ¼″ clothesline for a handle

Old-time carpenters used to carry their tools in a carrier like this. You can also use it for gardening tools, hobby equipment, or boxes of hardware like nails and screws.

The carrier shown was made from 1″ x 8″. You might want to make yours from 1″ x 6″, which will make it slightly smaller, but also easier to carry around. If your lumber yard carries lumber ½″ thick in the width you need (either 8″ or 6″), you can make the two side pieces with that. This will make the carrier even lighter.

Begin by cutting your bottom piece to length, 18″. Now cut your ends, 11″. You'll notice that the end pieces taper toward the top. To make this taper, first find the center at the top of one end piece. Mark off ½″ on either side of this mark. This means that the top of the taper will be 1″ across.

Now place one end against the bottom, as shown. Put in place a piece of wood from which you will cut the sides. Draw lines from the sides to the upper marks on the end pieces. Cut the tapers and smooth with your plane.

Now drill the ¼″ holes for the rope handle in the very center of the end pieces, and 1″ down from the top. As shown in the photographs on page 17, make each ¼″ hole in two stages. First make a ⅛″ hole, then enlarge that hole with your ¼″ bit. That's a lot easier than trying to use the ¼″ bit right from the start.

Nail the ends to the bottom with 8-penny common nails. You'll probably need a helper to assemble the rest of the carrier. Mark off the thickness of the ends and bottom on your sides. Drive the nails on your work surface until they just start to come through. Then, with your helper holding the sides in position, drive the nails all the way in. This completes the building of the carrier.

Paint or stain the carrier. *After* that is done, put the ¼" clothesline through the holes and tie knots at either end. If the rope is hard to get through the holes, cut one end at a sharp angle with scissors, and it will pass through more easily.

This handy carrier is made of 1" x 8", although 1" x 6" may also be used. Parts are: two ends, 11" long; one bottom, 18" long; two sides, 19½" long. Don't cut the sides until the ends are attached to the bottom. Then check your measurements. Plus twenty-four 8-penny common nails and 26" of ¼" clothesline rope for a handle.

First cut bottom to length, 18″. Then cut end pieces. To mark off the hole for the rope, find center of the end and make a mark. Now measure 1″ down. Drill your hole where the lines cross. To find taper lines, position the bottom, end, and side pieces as shown, and draw lines. See text on page 48.

Saw diagonal cuts on taper lines in end pieces. Smooth with plane.

Line up both ends, hold in place with C-clamp, and drill through them at the same time. Use a ⅛″ bit first, then the ¼″ bit, as shown in the photographs on page 17.

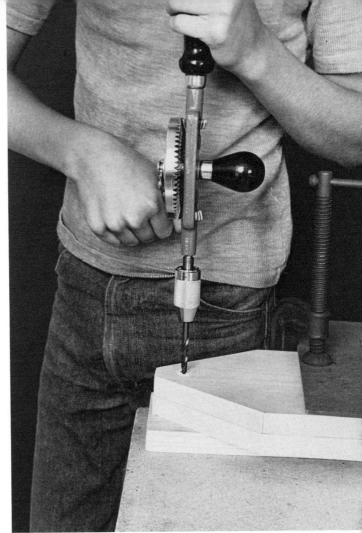

Attach the ends to the bottom with three 8-penny common nails. Do not hammer them all the way in until you're sure of the fit.

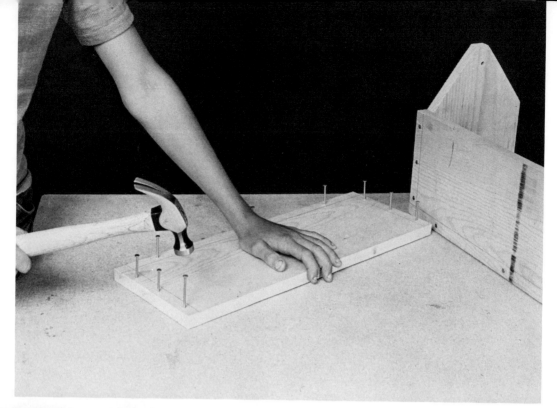

After marking off your thickness lines, hammer the nails into the side pieces until the points just start coming through the other side. Keep your holding hand away from the hammer.

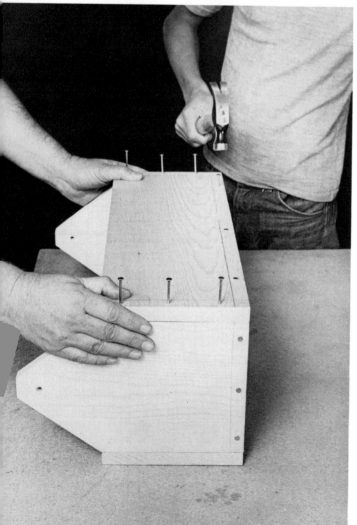

While your helper holds the side pieces in place, attach the sides to the bottom and ends.

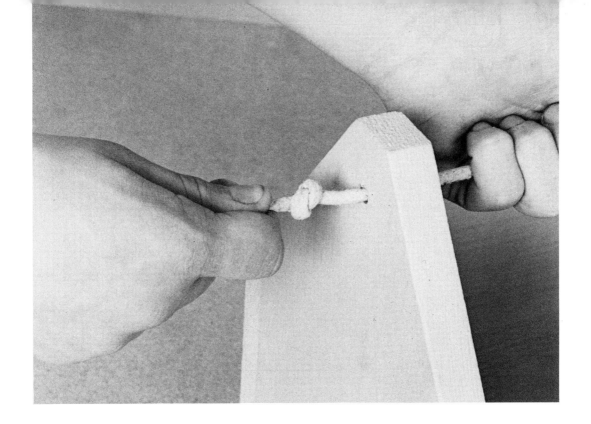

After you've painted or stained your carrier, put the rope through both holes and tie knots as close to the wood as you can. Don't do this *before* you finish the carrier or the paint or stain will soil the rope.

Reversible Shelf

In this position, without clothes hooks, the shelf is a great place to store books, plants, toys, your lunch box, or a radio.

In this position (inset), the shelf, with three clothes hooks, is a handy place to hang jackets and raincoats.

Lumber
1″ x 8″
    2 long pieces, 23″ each
    2 ends, 7¾″ each, from 10″ pieces
Total Lumber
66″

Fastening
5 8-penny common nails
8 6-penny finishing nails
glue

Hardware
2 screw eyes
3 clothes hooks
   (if used as clothes hanger)
2 picture hangers,
    30-pound capacity each

You can use this clever design two ways. Put three clothes hooks into it, and you've made a handy hanger, with its own top shelf for books and a lunch box. Or turn it upside down and you've made a shelf for books, toys, or a radio.

No matter how you use the shelf, your building steps are the same. You make the shelf of four pieces of 1″ x 8″—two long pieces and two end pieces. Begin by cutting your two long pieces to size—23″ long. Nail the two together, as shown on page 58 (top) with 8-penny common nails. Check the joint with your try square. You'll notice that when you join pieces in this way, although they are both 1″ x 8″, one surface becomes deeper than the other.

Now you're ready to measure and cut your end pieces. Put the nailed-together long pieces on your work table, as shown on page 58 (bottom). Hold a 10″ length of 1″ x 8″ flush against one edge. Notice the direction of the wood grain. Mark off the ends of the nailed-together section, and then draw your diagonal line. Do this for both end pieces.

Cut and plane the end pieces. Start driving your 6-penny finishing nails while the end pieces are resting on your work surface. Then have your helper hold them in position, and begin nailing them in place. Do not hammer them all the way in until you are sure they are placed exactly right. For more strength, use glue to join the ends to the long section.

If you want to use the shelf as a hanger, mark off your hanger positions on the part of the L that is less deep. This will give you a deeper top shelf, where you really need more space.

Now make starter holes for your clothes hangers. (If you can't find the type of hanger shown, you may use metal or wooden drawer pulls. Drill ⅛″ holes and attach the pulls with the screws that come with them.) The hooks are all 3½″ from the bottom edge. The middle hook is in the center of the board, 11½″ from either end. The end hooks are 4½″ from each end. Make your pencil marks at these measured points and tap an 8-penny common nail lightly into your pencil marks.

Now make starter holes for the hook eyes that will hold your shelf on the wall. These holes are located 2″ from the ends. Again, use an 8-penny common nail and make your starter holes toward the back edge of the wood, so that your shelf will hang flat against the wall.

Do not attach any hardware until your shelf has been painted or stained. When the paint or stain dries, screw in the clothes hangers and screw eyes. Hammer two picture hooks into your wall, making sure they are level. Then hang up your shelf!

The entire shelf is 1″ x 8″. The long pieces are 23″. The ends are cut from 10″ pieces.

Use 8-penny common nails for the long pieces, 6-penny finishing nails for the ends.

Above: Begin by starting your common nails on your work surface. Then, while your helper holds both pieces in the correct position, hammer the nails all the way in.

Below: Notice that although both pieces are 1" x 8", one side of the L is deeper. Hold one 10" piece as shown and mark off the ends. Then connect your marks with the diagonal line. Notice the direction of the grain when working with each piece.

Above: Cut the end pieces and start your nails on your work surface. Spread a thin coating of glue on the ends of the long pieces. When the pieces are perfectly in place, begin hammering in your 6-penny finishing nails.

Below: If you're going to use the shelf to hang clothes, mark off the positions of your hooks—the middle one is 11½" from each end; the end ones are 4½" in. Make starter holes with an 8-penny common nail. All hooks are 3½" in from the bottom edge.

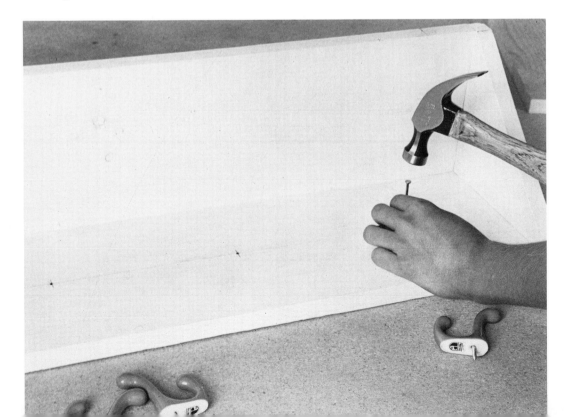

Your starter holes for the screw eyes are also made with an 8-penny common nail. The holes are 2″ from each end and toward the back edge of the wood.

Below left: This is the position for the screw eye when you use the shelf with clothes hooks. The narrower side of the L is against the wall. The shelf is hung up with two picture hooks, which you can buy in any five-and-dime. To be safe, buy picture hooks that will support 30 pounds each.

Below: This is the position of the screw eye that hangs the shelf when you use it for books. The wider side of the L is flat against the wall.

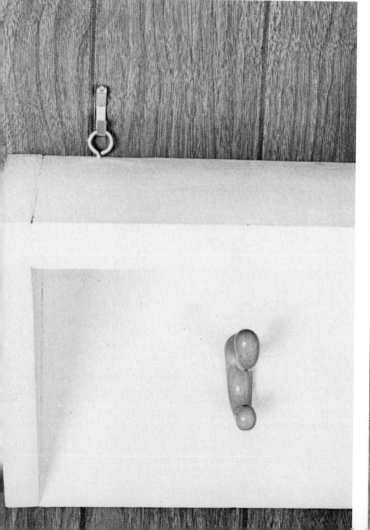

To use the shelf for clothes hooks, screw in a colored porcelain hook like the center one. Or use wooden or metal drawer pulls for "hooks." They are perhaps easier to find and will work well, too.

Pet Bed

It's a lot nicer than a cardboard box, and your cat or dog will love it. The front corners of both side pieces have been tapered off. A piece of carpet cut to size makes the pet bed even more comfortable. If you have a large pet, you can make the floor deeper by using 1″ x 10″ for the floor instead of 1″ x 8″.

Lumber

1″ x 8″ for the floor
   2 pieces, 15″ each
1″ x 6″ for the back and sides
   2 sides, 14½″ each (or as long
     as the floor is deep)
    1 back, 16½″
2″ x 3″ for runners
   2 pieces, 14½″ each

Total lumber

1″ x 8″ — 30″
1″ x 6″ — 45½″
2″ x 3″ — 29″

Fastening

28 6-penny common or
   finishing nails
glue

You can make your dog or cat a bed of its very own. The floor of the pet bed shown is made of 1″ x 8″ lumber. It measures 15″ wide by 14½″ deep. This is a good size for a small cat or dog. If your pet is larger, you can make the floor of the bed bigger in two ways. First, you can still use 1″ x 8″ but cut it more than 15″ long. Second, you can make the bed deeper as well as longer. Just use 1″ x 10″ and cut it more than 15″. If you make the floor larger, the sizes of the sides and back will also have to be larger, so remember that.

To find out how big *your* pet's bed should be, measure the space your cat or dog takes up while he's lying down. Then build the bed to his own measurements. Allow several extra inches on all sides so that he can fit comfortably.

Begin by cutting your two floor boards to length. Place the floor boards side by side on your 2″ x 3″, so that they are flush on one end. Mark off this measurement, then cut your 2″ x 3″ to size. Cut the second 2″ x 3″ to size, using the first as a measure.

Nail the floor boards to the 2 x 3's with 6-penny finishing nails or common nails. This completes the floor.

The sides and back are made of 1″ x 6″. The sides are as long as the floor is deep. In this case, 14½″. Cut both side pieces. Now cut the sharp front corners off the side pieces. Measure 1″ down at the front and 3″ in from the end to make the angle. Make your cuts, then smooth the slopes down with your plane. Now you're ready to join the sides to the floor.

But before starting each nail, you want to make sure of one thing: that the nails in your sides will not hit the nails that hold the floor boards to the 2 x 3's. To avoid this, hold a side piece in place as shown on page 68 (top). Mark crosses for your nails, making sure these crosses miss the nails already driven.

Start driving each nail on your work surface until the point starts coming through. Then, as your helper holds the floor upright, finish nailing both sides. *Make sure both rounded corners are facing the same direction before you start nailing.*

With the sides attached, all you need to add to the bed is the back. Measure the distance across the back and cut your back piece to size. Again, start all your nails on your work surface. When the nail points start coming through, nail the back to the side pieces. And that's your pet bed.

The bed shown was painted dark blue. When the paint was dry, a piece of carpet was cut to fit and put in place. You can also use a folded blanket or pillow.

Materials from bottom to top. Runners: two pieces of 2″ x 3″, each 14½″ long. Floor: two pieces of 1″ x 8″, each 15″ long. Back: one piece of 1″ x 6″, 16½″ long (but do not measure or cut the back until the sides are nailed on). Sides: two pieces of 1″ x 6″, each 14½″ long. Glue is used to help hold the sides to the floor pieces, and you can use either 6-penny common or finishing nails.

Begin by cutting your floor boards to length —15" long for the bed shown (but make yours longer if your pet needs more room). Position the floor boards as shown and mark your 2 x 3's for cutting. Floor boards should be level. Use books or scrap wood to prop floor boards up until both 2 x 3's are cut.

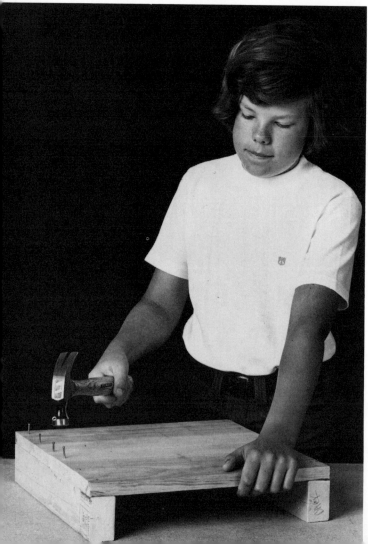

After both runners are cut, attach the floor boards to the runners. You can use either 6-penny common or finishing nails for this. Make sure the boards are where you want them before nailing all the way in.

Cut your side pieces to the proper length. The side pieces are as long as your floor is deep—in this case, 14½". Then make your marks for tapering the front corners— 1" down at the front, 3" in from the front. Draw your line and make your cut.

Smooth and round off the taper with your plane. Work on the edges of the wood as well as on the surface.

Before starting your nails in the side piece, hold the piece in place. Make crosses where your nails will go, spaced so that the new nails will not hit the nails in the floor boards.

Apply a thin coat of glue to the ends of the floor boards and the bottom of the side pieces. Attach the side pieces. Make sure that both tapered corners face in the same direction.

When measuring for your back piece, measure along the bottom. The tops of the sides may slant slightly in or out, so the bottom measurement is more accurate.

Start your nails on your work surface until the points start coming through. Then attach the back when you're sure everything is lined up correctly.

Wood Finishing

If you look around the house at your wooden furniture, you'll see that it has been covered with stain, varnish, or paint. These finishes seal and protect the wood and make the furniture look better. Raw wood, wood that is unfinished, quickly becomes dirty and hard to clean.

Here's how the projects in this book were finished:

Potholder Hanger: varnish stain; orange-brown; slightly glossy finish; two coats.

Book Rack: Minwax finish; light brown; dull finish; one coat.

Hanging Planter: exterior wood preservative; light green; dull finish; two coats.

Handy Carrier: undercoat; yellow latex; flat finish; two coats.

Reversible Shelf: undercoat; yellow latex; flat finish; two coats.

Pet Bed: white shellac to cover knots so they do not "bleed" through the paint and leave brown spots; undercoat; blue latex; flat finish; two coats.

This does not mean that you have to finish your own projects exactly as shown. It may depend on what kind of paints you happen to have in your basement, or how you want the job to look.

Staining is easiest, because you just brush it on, and that's it. Painting is more difficult, because if you want to do a good job, you should first cover any knots with white shellac. Then use a white undercoat, and then two coats of your color. Painting takes the most time and most effort. Every coat should be allowed to dry thoroughly before applying the next. To be safe, allow each coat to dry overnight.

Regardless of *how* you finish your projects, there are some general rules.

- Your work should be sanded down smoothly. Remove all pencil marks by rubbing your sanding block vigorously over them. If you can do the sanding outside, you're better off—a driveway or porch is fine, as long as the dust isn't inside. If you have to sand and paint in the same room, the sanding dust will stay in the air for a long time, even if you can't see it. Then as your paint is drying, the dust will stick to the wet paint and make a rough surface. So do your sanding *away* from where you do your painting.

- Before you start finishing, be sure you have everything you'll need: old newspapers; empty cans or cut-down milk cartons to hold stain or paint; brushes; paint stirrers; rags to wipe up spills; and, very important, some old clothes. One of your father's old shirts makes a fine painter's smock. Cut the sleeves short so they won't get in the way.

- Never stain or paint anything that's sitting directly on your work surface. Protect the surface with newspapers. And always rest your work on a couple of pieces of scrap. In this way, you can paint all the way to the bottom, and the project won't stick to anything as it dries.

- Don't see how much paint or stain you get on at once. Dip your brush only halfway into your paint, wipe off the excess paint on the rim of the can, and use slow, steady strokes. Move your brush *with* the wood grain. If you use stain, try it on a test piece of scrap first to see what color you'll get. Stain is very watery. You need very little on your brush at a time. Keep a rag handy for spills and to wipe off excess stain.

- Be patient. Once you have painted or stained a piece of wood, leave it alone until the finish dries. Don't keep touching the surface with your finger to see if it is dry. Paint the work and forget it. If the finish needs little touch-ups, make them later on.

- Take care of your brushes. Brushes used for stain may be cleaned out with turpentine, wiped clean with a rag, and then hung up to dry. The used rags should be thrown into *covered metal containers.* The rags should never be left in the work room. Brushes used for latex paint can be washed out easily with just soap and warm water.

Basic supplies for wood finishing: Newspapers to protect your work surface. Empty cans and a cut-down milk carton for holding small amounts of paint. Rags to wipe up spills or to remove excess stain. Brushes. White shellac to cover wood knots (if you paint over knots without shellacking first, the knots will "bleed" through the finish). Paints and stain. Sandpaper block and two grades of sandpaper, medium and fine. You can make your own sandpaper block by tacking sandpaper around a block of wood.

All projects should be sanded down smoothly first, using medium-grade sandpaper and then fine-grade. If you do this outside, there will be less mess to clean up.

Varnish stain darkens the wood of the pot-holder hanger and also gives it a slight shine. This color is a rich orange-brown, called Cape Cod Maple. All projects should rest on pieces of scrap while they are being finished. This lets you paint right down to the bottom without having the project stick to the newspaper.

The book rack was finished with one coat of Minwax Ipswich Pine. Unlike the varnish stain, this leaves a dull finish.

Because the planter will be kept outside,
it needs a special finish called an *exterior*
stain. This stain is made to protect things
that are kept out of doors. The finish used
was pale green, but other colors are available.

Before the pet bed was painted, the wood
knots were covered with white shellac.

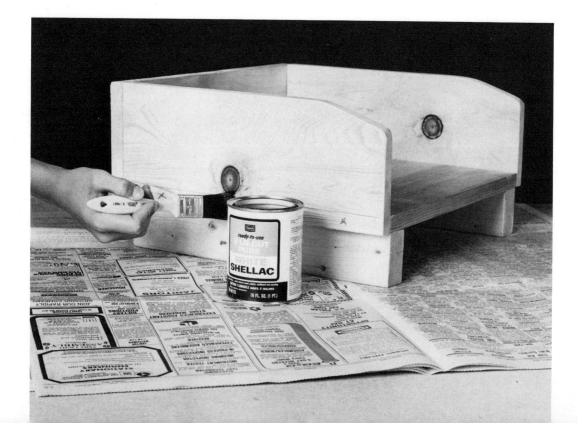

The pet bed gets a white undercoat before its final blue color. This undercoat will hide many of the smaller knotholes and nail holes. Stain makes the grain show up more, but paint covers and seals the wood completely. Let each coat dry overnight.

This is the first of two coats of latex paint used on the pet bed. When completely dry, the second coat will be applied.

Acknowledgments

Although this book bears only one name as its author, it was really a group effort. I would like to express my gratitude to: my friend David Eynon for his invariably helpful suggestions during the writing; Jeff Murphy, who shot and processed all the clear, explanatory photographs; the children who posed for the pictures—Peter Surette, Julie and David Wiesner, and my daughter Lisa; my son David for toting stuff to and from the studio; my daughter Louise for her help in proofreading; my wife Lee for naming the book; my agent Harriet Wasserman for suggesting the project in the first place; and the staff at Dutton—Ann Troy, Riki Levinson, and Susan Shapiro—for their many contributions to the finished work.